Women on View

A play by
ROY RUSSELL

SAMUEL   FRENCH

LONDON
NEW YORK TORONTO SYDNEY HOLLYWOOD

MADE AND PRINTED IN GREAT BRITAIN BY
LATIMER TREND AND COMPANY LTD PLYMOUTH
MADE IN ENGLAND

CHARACTERS

Jo Cox
Props Girl

Jackie Gill
Floor Manager

Ruth Delahay
Producer/Director

Shirley Whitridge
Television personality

Edna Morton-Smith
Novelist

Wendy Stamford
Production Assistant

Caroline Power
Anchor-woman of "Women On View"

Jean Redding
"Special Guest" Viewer

Susanna Frank
Character Actress

The action passes in a television studio

Time – the present

The first performance of *Women on View* was given by the Drama Group of Bookhams Evening Women's Institute on 24th May 1973 in the Barn Hall at Great Bookham, Surrey.

PRODUCTION NOTES

With the exception of Jean Redding, all the characters are "professionals", talking about their work and performing their jobs, experienced to the level of doing so seemingly effortlessly. This makes Jean Redding the odd-woman-out, which adds to the theme of the play. She never shakes off the strong feeling that a TV studio is a tricky place where the uninitiated could easily do the wrong thing and cause trouble, even if only technical. The professionals cannot help looking upon her as not of their esoteric world. Even though they go out of their way to disguise this, it still shows.

"V.T.R." stands for Video Tape Recording, the process by which most television productions are pre-recorded, in sound and vision, for transmission at a later date. When a studio problem arises the tape may be stopped and wound back or left running for subsequent editing.

"Telecine" is the apparatus which transfers any clip of pre-shot film on to the video tape being used to record the studio sequences at the desired moment it has to be inserted. For example, the titles and background shots which begin the programme every week viz. "WOMEN ON VIEW" and "Introduced by Caroline Power".

"Ident" is short for future identification of the video-tape, a verbal label spoken by the Floor Manager during the final count-down.

The "script" referred to is a format of the programme and does not contain any of the discussion which is extemporized during the recording.

ROY RUSSELL

WOMEN ON VIEW

The following detailed description of the stage setting re-creates a small television studio. If staging facilities and resources are very limited, the setting may be suggested quite simply with five chairs and a low-table without any scenery whatsoever

The scene throughout is part of a small television studio used for interviews, current affairs programmes and "chat shows", like the one for which it is at present set: the popular afternoon programme "Women On View". The studio wall is represented by the actual hall or theatre back-wall. Three or four garden-hose-like black cables snake across the floor, possibly "bridged across" by a striped wooden ramp to prevent their being tripped over. A few steps and a tubular rail are all we see of a staircase which leads eventually up to the Control Gallery. Off L are unseen double-doors which lead out of the studio at floor-level. Three unseen television cameras are imagined to be roaming in the auditorium, but using their long-range lenses for close-ups

The television setting for "Women on View" is a simple backing of flats or screens, rather like a stage inset, in pastel shades to create an attractive background. On it is a motif of "Women on View" (see TV chat shows for examples). The studio wall behind can be seen above and at the sides of the "set", in front of which is a slightly curved row of five decorous chairs, the middle one being slightly superior. There is room between the chairs and the backing for studio staff to have access for adjustments to hair styles or whatever, when required. In front of the centre three chairs is an equally decorous (but unfussy and non-masking) low table and two microphones, non-practical, from which cables lead off under the set, as if to control-points in the back wall. On the table is a letter, a few researchers' notes, and a brand new copy of the novel "Love Is A Shallow Grave" by Edna Morton-Smith. Off the set to L is a cheap but sturdy small table carrying a few spare scripts (say ten pink pages of A4 each), and a tatty G.P.O. black telephone marked with a band of red sticky-tape on both base and handset for identification. Down L *is a monitor, like an old domestic TV set, facing the chairs. Its close-circuit cable snakes off* L

The studio set is not yet lit for cameras, but the overall studio-lighting is very adequate for all other purposes

Jo Cox, the props "girl", sharp, used to reacting quickly and silently, in old jeans, sneakers and a man's patterned shirt, carries a script on a clip-board, which she temporarily puts down on the table whilst she picks up the envelope, rehearses smartly taking out the letter so that it comes out the right way up to be read immediately. Then she returns it to the envelope ensuring it is correctly folded to come out right next time. The Floor Manager, Jackie Gill, comes in from the studio doors, an ex-actress who was not good-looking enough to make the grade whilst young and who eventually refused to settle for being more out of work than in, and now committed to a full-time job in television production. She has just clipped her neck-mike, the size of a stubby lipstick case, on to her shirt-blouse. It is connected by thin flex to a portable transmitter (a grey box the size of a small box of chocolates and dangling a short aerial-lead) which she slips in the hip-pocket of her jeans. Then she places the earpiece, like an undisguised hearing-aid, in her ear, as she has done many times. She concentrates absolutely on her very responsible role as boss of the studio floor, even when she is being jokey with unseen male technicians. Whilst she is fitting her equipment she speaks, checks the set, chairs, etc., approves Jo's final adjustments, and checks her watch

Jackie Oh, check that letter comes out right way round. You know what a fuss she made last week.

Jo Just done it. Any more news?

Jackie Yes, she's on her way. We're going up soon as she's with us.

Jo She'll be okay to do the show, will she?

Jackie You *know* Caroline Power. Professional from her finger-nails to her contact lenses. Oh, nip up to the gallery, Jo; ask "Sound" for a neck-mike for Caroline, will you?

Jo A neck-mike? (*Indicating the stand-mikes*) Aren't we using these, this week?

Jackie Last thing she said after the last recording. She wants one every week. Tell Roger it doesn't have to be practical. She doesn't need the transmitter box, just a mike.

Jo What's the point then?

Jackie How should I know? Puts her one up on the Panel, I suppose. You know what they say, it's the badge of the most exclusive club in the world.

Jo (*indicating Jackie's mike*) And you're a member.

Jackie I'm never seen on camera, that's the difference.

Jo If *you*'d made the big time, Jackie, would you have played up like that?

Jackie We'll never know. I'm not sorry I gave up acting. Caroline's not bad, compared with some I could name.

Jackie concentrates on making her earpiece comfortable and effective. She speaks quite normally as if to someone just in front of her

   Jo goes off up to the gallery

Jackie Hearing me okay, gallery? (*She looks up high in the direction of the gallery*) Yes, receiving you super. Is Rodge there? (*Listens*) Rodge; Jo's on her way up for a neck-mike for Caroline. (*Listens*) We all know she doesn't *need* one, darlin'. She *wants* one, and that's *it*. (*Listens*) Well, get one from somewhere, or Caroline'll hit the roof. Thanks. (*Listens*) Yes, Jock? (*Listens*) The latest *I've* heard is Caroline's sent word she's on her way; I don't think we'll be starting V.T.R. more than about ten minutes behind schedule so light as soon as you want to. (*Listens*) No, we don't know any more than was in the paper this morning. And *I'm* not going to ask her, lovey; floor-manager jobs aren't easy come by at the moment and I like it here, didn't you know. (*Listens*) Yes, Adrian. (*Listens*) Which one? (*She goes to the end chair on the* R) Don't say "viewer's" chair. Didn't you get Ruth's memo? (*Slightly adjusts chair in line*) That okay? (*Listens*) The viewer-guest is to be referred to at all times as the "Special Guest". (*Listens*) I love you too, Adrian, but don't tell your wife.

The banter is shot from Jackie's mind by the arrival from the studio doors of Ruth Delahay, Producer/Director of "Women on View", dressed trendily in good taste and quality and very practical for "studio day", quietly authoritative, firmly the boss.

She escorts Shirley Whitridge, a well-known telly-performer and columnist, sophisticated, confident and subtly superior about her on-the-box track-record; and Edna Morton-Smith, novelist and professional intellectual, introspective until emotionally worked-up, strikingly dressed but not outlandish.

They are followed by Wendy Stamford, the Production Assistant (a stop-watch slung from her neck on a black tape), attractive although bespectacled; serious-minded, on the "qui vive" to anticipate Ruth's requirements in any situation; always at her elbow, but unobtrusive unless needed. Ruth carries a script by its stapled corner; Wendy's is on a clip-board across her forearm and is book-marked with stapled paper tabs, one of which she uses as a reference to whisper a minor detail change to Jackie. Ruth shows Shirley and Edna where they will sit

Ruth Shirley. On Caroline's left, please.

Shirley Fine, wherever you say.

Ruth Miss Morton-Smith on Caroline's right.

Edna I don't mind being on the end. Won't Miss Franks want to sit next to Caroline Power?

Ruth That's exactly what that po-faced twit who runs her would insist on if I let him. But no-one dictates terms on this show. Not even Susanna Frank's personal manager.

Shirley Her own manager, that *is* success.

Ruth Oh, she doesn't admit to being a television actress any more; she's a film-star. But I ban personal managers from the studio, and she's throwing a last-minute temperament because I won't let him hold her hand until we start recording. Don't worry, Jackie, it'll all be over before we go up, you'll see.

Shirley (*smiling*) Or she never works for you again, eh?   *now*

Stronger lighting now illuminates the setting and chairs

Ruth You have done other chat-shows, haven't you, Miss Morton-Smith?

Edna Oh, yes. But I'm not in the same league as Miss Whitridge.

Ruth (*partly joking*) Oh, *she's* beginning to suffer from over-exposure. When were you last on the box?

Edna Oh, heavens—"thinks". (*She does think*) Not since my last book. I talk better to my typewriter than on my feet. You can't rewrite something you've *said* rather badly.

Ruth Well, you'll find the cameras don't come in as tight on you as they used to. Nowadays we can pull a Big Close Up just by zooming the lens. Much less off-putting.

Shirley You'll forget they're there; I do.

Ruth looks out front

Ruth Camera Two; Jimmy, isn't it? Give me a tight close-up on Miss Morton-Smith, will you? (*She waits*) That it? Now, you're in Big Close Up—just eyebrows to nostrils. From that distance, see?

Edna What a revolting thought. But quite remarkable, I agree.

Shirley It's all done with mirrors. Great big cheat from start to finish. Cameras lie all the time.

Ruth But *we* don't. Whatever we say on camera must be factually accurate. We don't want letters complaining. Thanks, Jimmy love.

Shirley When I was in the House I voted against it. To have them eavesdropping during debates would give a completely wrong idea.

Edna There are two schools on that. I think people have a right to see exactly what goes on in Parliament.

Ruth But we won't debate it now. It's not germane to today's subject anyway.

Ruth looks at her watch

Shirley Ruth, if Caroline's too upset . . . You know, it could be pretty grim for her . . .

Ruth She'll make it. Thanks, Shirley, just the same.

Shirley If you want to suggest it, I'd willingly take over for her. Only this one show, of course.

Ruth smiles at Shirley's opportunism

Ruth Of course. Very kind Shirley. She'll get through. Nobody's more professional than Caro when the chips are down. Once we're recording, the show will be all she thinks about; you'll see.

Jackie presses her fingers to her earpiece

Jackie (*listening*) Reception just phoned the gallery. Caroline's coming through; said she isn't bothering going to Make-up.

Ruth (*approving*) That's Caro. Special Guest on the set, please, Wendy. And tell our temperamental young film lady we "V.T.R." in four minutes. Whether she's on the floor or not.

Wendy goes off fast, to the studio doors

Shirley I never knew Caroline was married to Bob Harvest until I saw the paper this morning.

Ruth She didn't talk about it as a rule.

Edna That's Robert Harvest, the film producer, is it? Do we know what happened?

Ruth Only snippets. Head-on crash with a lorry. His car was a write-off.

Shirley Is he *still* unconscious?

Ruth That's all they'd tell me. You know hospitals.

During the above Jo comes quietly down the gallery steps and moves behind the seats to put the neck-mike for Caroline on the table. Then she silently goes off R

Shirley Let's hope the fact Caroline is here means better news.

Ruth I wouldn't bet on it. She'd've got here if it killed her.

Edna May I ask? What is the significance of not meeting the housewife type until we . . .

Ruth "Special Guest", dear. Don't make that awful gaff on camera, whatever you do. We had awful trouble, oh three shows ago. Women's Lib type. Caroline called her "the viewer". What were we? Arrogant, superior, a coterie, cop-outs, a closed shop, an élite, living in a glass-bubble; you name it. This week's looks she'll be no trouble. But we have found in the past that if we invited the Special Guest to join us in the Hospitality Room she asked all her best questions there and we didn't get them on the show. It works better this way, you'll see.

Ruth moves towards Carline as she enters from the studio doors. They embrace, holding each other tightly for a moment. Caroline

breaks first. She is tense but covers her distress by putting a brave
face on when she speaks. Her subtly compelling speech, natural
sincerity and charm show why she has a successful TV show.
She dresses in a subtly striking way and makes the very best of
her looks; yet somehow she is aloof and alone

Caroline (*unstressed*) Sorry, everybody; so very sorry. Do forgive
me, please.

Shirley Caro, darling . . .

Shirley makes to move to her but Caroline restrains her before she
reaches her

Caroline (*still playing it down*) No, Shirley, I take everyone's
sympathies as read. I know they're there. Nice of you to come
on the show. (*To Edna*) Hallo. We've not worked together
before, have we? I'm afraid I haven't even glanced at your
new book. I was going to this morning. . . . Our researchers will
have. (*She picks up the notes from the table*) There you are,
they've *both* read it. (*She reads the note*) Fine. I can quote that,
nobody will be wiser. Good, where's Mrs Average Viewer,
Ruth?

Ruth Special Guest's on her way, Caro. (*She does not stress the*
correction with her star)

Caroline And where's our interpreter of licentious ladies,
Susanna Whatsit?

Ruth Last-minute second-thoughts about appearing if her
personal manager isn't just out of shot to wet-nurse her.

Caroline Maybe her head's so big she can't get through the studio
doors without scraping her ears.

Ruth I'm cutting her to size, don't worry.

Caroline I'd like to slip in a call to the hospital when you stop-
tape somewhere.

Ruth Of course. Is he still unconscious?

Caroline Not a flicker; am I all right without make-up? I did
a quick repair job in the car.

Ruth (*checking*) Fine. Super, in fact.

Caroline We're not going to *wait* for Miss Sexpot, are we? I'd
rather we grab a little actress from somewhere else in the
building. *Any* little actress. She doesn't have to say much, with
talent like this on either side of me.

Ruth (*smiling confidently*) Kika Bennett's standing by in Rehearsal Room Three. Drama say they're prepared to release her for an hour.

Caroline Does Susanna know that?

Ruth No, but she *will*, if she isn't here within two minutes. Ah, Mrs Redding, come along and meet everybody.

Wendy leads Jean Redding on to the side of the set and Ruth goes to her. She is dressed rather more for an occasion than the others on the panel, but does not feel this herself. She is uncertain rather than apprehensive and Ruth welcomes her more reassuringly than necessary

Ruth (*to Wendy*) Tell Susanna I've another actress standing by and the studio doors will be locked in two minutes.

Caroline With a red light over them.

Edna Might one add: appropriately?

Wendy goes off towards the studio doors

Ruth (*to Jean*) You said you haven't been in a studio before, didn't you? Well, don't worry about that; you've seen the show and this is where it happens, that's all there is to it. Caroline Power you know by sight.

Jean Of course.

Caroline shakes hands but her greeting is that touch overdone

Caroline Very nice of you to give up your time to come along and join us, Mrs . . .

Jean Redding.

Ruth Shirley Whitridge; and Edna Morton-Smith.

Shirley Hello.

Edna Hello.

Jean How d'you do.

They smile and nod but Ruth, instead of bringing Jean to them, ushers her off the set area

Ruth You know the format, do you? Our "Special Guest" is the only member of the panel to make an entrance. So you stand out of shot, here, until Jackie cues you.

Then all you do is walk on and sit down, on the end chair. (*Indicating the chair*) Then take your cue from Caroline; she's the boss, once we're on V.T.R.—sorry, when we're recording.

Jean I see. Thank you.

Jackie takes up a position slightly behind Jean

Ruth Don't give a thought to the cameras. You won't know they're there. Concentrate entirely on what you're saying and you'll come over splendidly.

Jean I see. Yes.

Ruth Is there anything you're not sure of?

Jean No, I don't think so. Except perhaps . . .

Ruth forgets Jean as Susanna Franks enters. She looks her age in her face but is physically younger. She has been a television actress playing intense emotional parts but has just had her first feature-film success playing an earthy part which got favourable notices. She is going through a phase of feeling rather more important than she really is, yet underlying is an insecurity. She uses her eyes well and wears a provocative dress, knowing just how far she can go in a chat-show. Ruth rocks the boat for the show's sake, but only very gently

Ruth Susanna, dear. Just made it. Well done.

Susanna Sorry, my hair wasn't quite right and Wolfie, my personal manager, had this call from New York. I can't talk about it, because nothing's signed yet, but it sounds exciting.

Caroline Not to worry, darling, we won't breathe a word on the show.

Jean is still temporarily forgotten

Susanna Oh hello, I'm so sorry about Bob's accident. What a dreadful thing.

Ruth We're trying not to talk about it.

Caroline We're definitely not talking about it. (*Putting her on*) You're *sure* you don't want me to mention this dramatic telephone call?

Susanna Well, it would be nice. But nothing's signed. If Wolfie were here I could ask him.

Ruth Yes, well, that's a pity, but he must stay in the viewing room.

Ruth takes her to the end seat L

Ruth You know Shirley Whitridge. Edna Morton-Smith. We're ready to go when you are.

There are smiles and nods across the chairs as Susanna sits

Susanna Oh, *I'm* ready. Terrified without a script. But ready.
Ruth Two minutes, Jackie.

Wendy crosses the set inobtrusively and goes up the steps to the gallery

Jackie Two minutes, studio, please.
Caroline Have you read Miss Morton-Smith's new book?
Susanna No. No, I'm sorry to say I haven't. Isn't that awful?
Shirley I don't suppose she's seen your film.
Edna No, I'm afraid not. It's only been out a few days, hasn't it?
Susanna The premiere was last Monday. Do see it, please.
Shirley Is it as good as the notices? Or did you bribe the critics?

Ruth is now sure of Susanna and turns back to Jean. Ruth glances at her script

Susanna Critics won't take money. I mean, I've never heard of an actress offering a bribe.
Shirley I wasn't thinking of money.

Ruth has been glancing at her script

Ruth From the top then. Nice and relaxed, everybody. Let it flow; just as it comes, no inhibitions about anything. I don't mind what you say so long as you disagree and argue. We can chop out any four-letter-word-stuff but we can't stick any in if you go all flat and dreary. You know what I mean. Good luck, everybody. (*As she goes to the gallery steps*) If we don't have to break, Caro, I'll give you a tape-stop about half-way, that all right? (*Pointing to the telephone*) Jackie, is that through to the gallery? Or the switchboard?
Jackie Switchboard. Outgoing calls only.
Ruth Take it there then, Caro.

Caroline Thank you, Ruth. Good luck to you, too. Good luck, everybody.

Ruth goes off up to the gallery

Caroline picks up her neck-mike and puts it on

Jackie (*very calm but firm*) Stand by studio, sixty seconds.

Caroline is adjusting the mike on her chest when she notices it is dusty. Not that anyone else could see

Caroline Oh, *no*. Where's this damn thing been? It's filthy.

Caroline indicates the minute dust on her fingertip. Jackie dashes up to see

Jackie (*calling*) Props!—"Sound" had to draw it from stores.
Caroline (*her pent-up tension momentarily bursting through*) Didn't anyone think to *clean* it?

Jo dashes in, taking out her handkerchief. She picks up the mike from Caroline's chest and carefully wipes the dust into her handkerchief

Jackie (*to her own mike*) Yes, Ruth, we're just . . . Okay now?

Jo finishes the dusting and dashes off

Caroline adjusts the mike and nods at Jackie

Ready when you are . . . Tape running. Thirty seconds . . . Ident: "Women On View"; Programme Forty-three; Take One. (*She pauses. Calmly*) Stand by, everyone.
Caroline (*to Shirley only, but not in a whisper*) How's Richard?
Shirley I've left him. At long last.
Caroline Somebody said they thought you had. Not before time, eh?
Shirley Five years' hell. Never again.
Susanna You will mention my film, won't you? Wolfie only let me do the show provided . . .
Jackie (*cool, but firm*) Quiet, please, tape's running, we're recording . . . (*She listens and repeats the gallery count down*) Ten seconds.

*In the tense silence Jackie kneels down out of shot, raises her arm,
and points her index finger towards Caroline, who keeps her
eyes on it*

Five: four: three. (*Three seconds pause*) We're on opening
title.   MUSIC

*The panel watch the titles appear on the monitor; then Jackie cues
Caroline with a sharp downstroke of her finger. Caroline's face
brightens, no stress now apparent. She speaks very relaxed and
with great charm into the unseen camera in the centre of the
auditorium*

Caroline Hello. Welcome again to "Women On View". Most of
you will know by now that each week we take a theme chosen
by you, the viewers, and try to . . .

Jackie Sorry, we've stopped. Yes, Ruth? (*She presses her earpiece as she listens*) Right. Not to worry, tape's still running.
Again from the top, please.

Caroline What was it? Not me?

Jackie No, cross-fade from titles not quite spot-on.

Caroline Was the level all right?

Jackie Sound? . . . Voice-level was fine? Stand by. And . . .

Jackie cues as before, Caroline reacts as before

Caroline (*just as fresh*) Welcome again to "Women On View". I'm
sure that if I just introduce my guests . . . No, I'm sorry, it
was better the first time. Could we go again?

Jackie (*on instructions*) Still running. *Quiet*, Studio. Here we go
again. And . . .

Jackie cues as before

Caroline (*still very fresh*) Welcome again to *Women On View*.
Most of you will know that our theme each week is chosen by
one of our viewers. But you may not guess our subject for
today, from my choice of guests. Shirley Whitridge, one-time
Member of Parliament, lecturer and one of the best-known
faces on television. The novelist Edna Morton-Smith whose
enthralling new book—(*an almost imperceptible glance at the
research notes*)—"Love is a Shallow Grave" is a searching if
rather cynical examination of—well, I won't say because that

does give away our theme. It's published by Flecker and Borg at two-pounds-twenty. And the actress who gave many superb performances in television plays, and is now collecting rave notices in the new film "Woman in Torment", Susanna Franks. And our Special Guest, whose letter was chosen out of hundreds. May I introduce——

Jo seems to materialize from nowhere with a cue-board which she holds just out of shot for Caroline, who reads it without giving that impression to the camera

—from Chilford, the wife of a Sales Director with two children: Peter, fourteen, and Marie, eleven—Mrs Jean Redding.

During this Jackie returns to Jean and unnecessarily holds her arm. Now she gently propels her towards the set, indicating the end chair without getting herself into shot

Jo disappears off R *with the cue-board*

Jean sits down rather stiffly and tries to relax. The lights slightly bother her, but she soon gets used to them

Welcome to "Women On View" Mrs Redding.

Jean Thank you.

Caroline I'm sure you recognize everybody on the panel?

Jean Mrs Whitridge and Miss Franks I've seen, yes. And there's a photo of Miss Morton-Smith on the back of her new book.

Edna You've read it?

Jean When I knew you were going to be on the panel, it was the first thing I did.

Caroline Now there's a real fan for you.

Jean I'm afraid I haven't read any of your other books.

Caroline Well, that may be a good place to start our discussion. (*To the centre camera*) But first, Mrs Redding's letter. (*She picks up the envelope and takes out the letter*) I won't read it all because you do go on a bit, don't you?

Jean Well, yes, I feel fairly strongly—you know.

Caroline This is the part. (*Reading the actual letter*) "What worries me in this day and age is the marriage contract. When people agree to any *other* sort of contract—to buy a house, or to make a business agreement, for example, the parties know what the contract means. What their benefits are, what their responsibilities are, what is expected of them under the contract they have signed. But nowadays everyone seems to have a different idea of what the marriage contract means. Is it not time that the contract between husband and wife was clearly defined in terms of today, so that those entering into such a contract know what they are engaging themselves for?" Yes. What made you suggest this theme, Mrs Redding?

Jean Well—I've seen what's happened to one of my friends recently. They'd been married for years. Children growing up. Then—trouble; and it's all over. One's always hearing of broken marriages these days.

Caroline Shirley Whitridge? Do we need a new marriage contract?

Shirley Well, I do see what Mrs Redding is driving at. Many of us have signed marriage contracts; and we all have trouble with the small print. Isn't that your point, Mrs Redding?

Jean Well, it's a question, really; I don't know the answer. I'm not suggesting we need a *new* marriage contract. Only that— that, er . . . (*She cannot find the words*)

Caroline Edna Morton-Smith?

Edna Compelling everyone to read the small print would be an excellent idea. You know the insurance joke about being covered for fire *and* theft. But when your house is burgled, because it wasn't on fire at the time, you have no claim. You should have been covered for fire *or* theft. Don't we need that sort of man's logic in marriage arrangements?

Susanna Oh, it wouldn't make men behave any better. If there were some sort of rule-book. They don't even stick to the "love and honour" bit.

Jean Oh, I don't think we can generalize. Some husbands do.

Susanna None that I meet, do, love.

Shirley I could mention a goodly number who *don't*, too.

Edna I think fewer people would rush into the marriage contract if their attention was drawn to a load of small print.

Caroline Susanna Franks? Fewer people rushing into marriage?

Susanna I once played a girl who jumped in with both feet. She was absolutely wrong for this lovely man, and at the end, after he'd killed himself, she was about to do the same to his younger brother. Hadn't learned a thing. Super play, lovely part.

Edna I'll bet it was written by a man.

Susanna Yes, it was. I nearly married him myself.

Shirley What stopped you?

Susanna I was already married unfortunately.

Shirley (*slightly superior*) Yes, well, isn't it a question of education? Young people should be given instruction on the traps and dangers.

Edna "Traps" is the operative word. Man-traps.

Susanna I played a girl who was miserable unless she was caught by a man. She wallowed in it, you know, she was that kind. Super part.

Jean But how *do* you teach young people to make sensible judgements. That only comes from experiencing life.

Caroline Aren't young people more sophisticated these days?

Jean I wasn't thinking about young people particularly. My letter is about people at any stage of their married lives.

Jackie comes forward into shot

Jackie Hold it there. (*She listens*) Sorry, someone's kicking the mike. (*She listens*) Mrs Redding, they think.

Jean Oh, I didn't know . . . so sorry.

Jackie goes to Jean

Jackie Yes, you only have to touch the base with your toe and it booms. Would you . . . ?

Jackie helps her move her legs so that her feet do not reach the mike-base

Jean Oh, I see. Sorry.

Jackie (*listening*) From where? . . . Yes, Ruth. (*To Caroline*) From your line "Aren't young people more sophisticated these days"?

Jean I said something after that. The point I wanted to make. About people at all stages of their married lives.

Jackie (*listening*) Yes, Ruth, will do. (*To Jean*) Sorry we can't pick it up there. It's a camera problem. We have to edit from suitable points. Tape's *still* running. (*Pointing at Caroline*) And . . .

Jackie cues Caroline

Caroline Aren't young people more sophisticated these days? Miss Morton-Smith, your new book—(*she picks it up*)—"Love is a Shallow Grave". Does the title have a bearing on this discussion?

Edna Well, yes, indeed it has. It is true, isn't it, that we *do* become buried by love. The point of the book is that we should . . . shake off the topsoil and get out of the grave we've dug ourselves into. Ergo, it is only a *shallow* grave.

Jean You can't generalize, surely?

Shirley But it is a general problem. Far too many people mix up love and marriage. Have some hidebound, traditional belief that the one only goes with the other.

Susanna Sure you can have love without marriage; and certainly marriage without love. I've played both parts.

Edna You can walk away from love outside of marriage without all those interminable legal wrangles. Heavens how they drag on; and *on*.

Jean I would have thought it would be just as hard to break a love-knot as the marriage-knot. If you were really in love. *More* difficult maybe.

Edna But you wouldn't *want* to, if you were *that* much in love. Although how many people are? They only *think* they are.

Jean But supposing the one you loved, er—no longer loved you. And *you* could no longer stand being ignored, walked over, used as a—housekeeper? Most of us, most people, live—well, straightforward lives; no glamour, no public limelight. What I hoped you could help me with is what should—should someone like my friend do? She needs help. Some sort of worthwhile advice, to help her save her marriage.

Susanna If it's smashed, why does she want to save it?

Edna Exactly. She's better to walk away from it.

Jean But supposing she can't?

Edna Has she told you she can't?

Jean Well, yes. She's tried. Several times.

Shirley She needs a push, that's all. It's like having a tooth out. More pain for a short while but no pain at all eventually.

Caroline Isn't she being selfish, your friend? Trying to hang on to a man who no longer loves her.

Jean No, she's not. She's not at all selfish. She's thinking of their children.

Caroline What ages are they?
Jean Ages? Er . . .

They begin to suspect that Jean may be talking about herself.
Caroline realizes that if this is so they may be in a tricky situation

Caroline If you'd rather not say for fear of identifying her to
viewers who may be friends of hers . . .
Jean Yes, I'd rather not. For that reason.
Shirley Could you put yourself in her shoes, Mrs Redding?
Jean How d'you mean?
Shirley If your husband no longer loved *you*—I mean, supposing
—would *you* tear up *your* marriage contract and walk out? Or
try to hold him to it?
Jean I—I don't know. It's difficult to say.
Caroline But it would help if you answered that question. Just
hypothetically. This is why we have viewer-participation on
this show. You yourself suggested *we* tend to live in a world
which is—well, not typical. Bounded by Fleet Street and
Westminster and the King's Road. What is the average housewife's thoughts on the subject, that is what matters, surely?
Jean I'm sorry. I never think of myself as "average" anything.
Caroline Well, a normal housewife.
Jean "Normal"—I probably *seem* normal to you, in *this* company. I don't think you *can* put people in pigeon-holes. The
man in the street; middle-class mothers; senior citizens. We're
not just a crowd of "Don't knows" in one of those polls; or
statistics in a Government report.
Shirley Surely people *do* fit into categories. By age, income-
bracket, occupation? Don't they?
Jean Does that mean we all have the same feelings? That we all
want the *same* out of life? I'm quite different from anyone
here, that's fairly obvious.
Edna In what *way* do you feel "different"?
Jean Not—different; that's not quite the word . . .
Caroline How do you see yourself; as an individual?

Jean feels she has nearly given herself away

Jean Well, I'm married—very happily married. I've been
luckier maybe or perhaps life isn't so hectic as it is with you.
I've two children I love more than anyth—that we *both* love

more than anything. But, you see, that was exactly the situation, until not very long ago, with my friend. Then she found . . . She began to realize that her marriage—that is her relationship with her husband—well, it had gone, it no longer existed. They didn't seem to *talk* about anything—or if they had to, like one of the children changing schools or something—it always ended in a row.

Caroline Is he unfaithful? Some other woman?

Edna His secretary, say? That's common enough.

Jean Not that I know . . . that *she* knows of. She has tried to find out.

Susanna No real communication; *I* know *that* scene.

Jean is now losing concentration of referring to "her friend"

Jean Now she realizes that everything she's striven for is—falling apart. And what can she do? You can't just walk out on your children, your friends. You don't want to lose any of it, not even *him*. If only he was like he was—once. But I can't go on just letting it go on . . .

Jean realizes she has shown that her "friend" is herself and is embarrassed. Jackie has received instructions and now comes forward, gently for Jean's sake. Caroline realizes they have stopped; drops her on-camera pose and goes to Jean

Caroline It's all right.

Jean You know, don't you? I'm not talking about . . . It's me; my *own* marriage . . .

Caroline Not to worry. (*To Jackie*) Ruth's cutting all that, is she?

Jackie is listening to her earpiece

Jackie Right, Ruth . . . Yes, we'll wipe all that, Mrs Redding, don't worry. Tape's stopped, Studio. We'll break for ten minutes, then pick up continuity. Ruth's coming down, Caroline.

Jean It's all been bottled up. There was nobody I could tell. Nobody. I'm sorry.

Caroline And that's why you wrote your letter; nobody blames you for that.

Jean I kept writing. Then tearing them up . . .

Ruth comes down from the gallery followed discreetly by Wendy with her script

Ruth (*calmly*) There's no panic; everybody relax. (*To Jean*) You've come through that pretty well; let me see. (*Ruth looks at Jean's face*) Haven't even messed up your face.

Jean I've messed up your programme, haven't I?

Caroline goes to Jackie's table and whispers to her. Jackie asks the switchboard for a number during the following

Ruth Not at all. It happens sometimes. Nothing we can't put right. All we do is rewind, and when we go again that last three minutes will be wiped clean.

Jean I wish I could wipe it clean out of my life.

Ruth (*regretfully*) We can only discuss problems. Never solve them.

Susanna Just like when you do a play. Doesn't help my problems ever.

Jean I was stupid to think you could help me.

Shirley It is a sort of electronic agony-column, isn't it? "Dear Auntie Television . . ."

Ruth We usually spot those letters and reject them.

Edna It's replacing the old parish priest, I suppose.

Jean I didn't mean you to know I was writing about myself. You see, I honestly didn't know who I could turn . . .

Ruth Caroline.

Ruth leaves Jean in mid-sentence as she sees Caroline on the telephone. She dashes over and cuts her off at the cradle. Jean is again forgotten

Caroline (*smiling*) D'you mind, Ruth? I'm phoning the hospital.

Ruth gently takes the telephone from her

Ruth (*as kindly as possible*) They rang through. I took it in the gallery. Whilst we were recording. Bob never came round. I'm sorry, Caro.

Caroline covers her reaction with a reproach

Caroline You—you let us run on? When you knew?

Ruth No point breaking-in, was there? It couldn't—change anything.

Caroline You could have—stopped, just to tell me. Then . . .

Ruth Wouldn't you rather have got the show in the can?

Caroline Did you think I might not see it through?

Ruth (*considerately*) I wouldn't have expected you to.

Caroline You mean the show's more important? Than that Bob's dead?

Ruth Not at all, Caro. I'm chopping the show right now. This one's a write-off.

Caroline (*not convincingly*) I'm willing to go on; if everyone else is?

Shirley Ruth's right, Caroline. It's not really on.

Edna I wouldn't want to either, in the circumstances.

Susanna (*sincerely*) The day my father died I had an "Armchair Theatre" to record. I was awful, I know I was.

Caroline I'm sorry, Ruth.

Caroline dashes off R

Ruth Try and get her to my office, Wendy. Give her a brandy. Anything she wants.

Wendy Yes, Ruth.

Wendy dashes off after Caroline

Jean Who is Bob, please?

Ruth Robert Harvest, the film producer.

Shirley He's Caroline's husband.

Jean Oh . . .

Ruth Break the studio, Jackie. VTR can wipe the tape.

Jackie That's it, everybody. Thank you very much.

Shirley Have you some shows in hand?

Ruth Three. None of them anything special. I'll put the best one out next week, not to worry. Damn!

The extra lighting on the setting is now killed leaving the studio evenly lit overall

Edna Ruth, would you mind terribly if I go?

Ruth No, there's nothing to stay for.

Jo comes on and silently clears props etc., in the background during the following. Jackie takes off her earpiece, neck-mike and transmitter

Edna Will you be doing this marriage theme again? It was going rather splendidly until er . . . And I thought my book fitted in, didn't it?

Ruth Well, yes, probably. Maybe—(*seeing that Jean is in earshot*) —not quite—in the same form. We'll see.

Edna Strange, isn't it. The way the very subject we were talking about blew up in our faces. My God, the things men do to us.

Shirley Oh, come on, he didn't smash himself up to ruin Caroline's programme.

Edna No, but what *speed* was he doing. Drive like nineteen-year-olds, some of them. I don't mind *him* killing himself but poor Caroline.

Ruth Don't worry. She'll survive.

Edna That's the nub of it, Ruth. We've no other choice but try to survive what men do to us.

Edna smiles bitterly and goes off R, *Jackie taking her as far as the studio exit*

Shirley Now I've a better idea why I've never been able to get on with her books.

Susanna Would you mind if I go too? Wolfie didn't really have time to explain that New York call. Oh, he's sure to ask me how this works out, I mean my contract to appear.

Ruth You'll be paid your fee in full. (*Slightly acid*) With my love, tell him.

Susanna Yes, yes, I will. Well, good-bye, everybody, it's been fun. I mean it would've been, wouldn't it? What a shame, on my first chat-show.

Jackie returns just in time to escort Susanna off to the studio doors

Shirley Not her last I don't suppose.

Jean is hanging back, uncertain whether to suggest she leaves, too

Ruth Some people never think of anyone but themselves.

Shirley Yes. You think Caroline'll be all right? In time for next week's recording, I mean?

Ruth I'm positive. She's a very tough lady, underneath.

Shirley I wonder how I'd've been if it had been Richard.

Ruth Is it true you've actually separated?

Shirley I couldn't stand any more. Even so it makes you wonder . . . Is that why you asked me on the show? Because you knew we'd split?

Ruth's smile is her answer

Shirley And Edna Morton-Smith? Earlier this year she washed all her dirty boy-friends in public. In that painful article. And Susanna keeps very quiet about that teenage son of hers.

Ruth Divorced at nineteen. Not bad going even for an actress.

Jean is listening, astonished at how the panel was chosen

Shirley I think you chose this week's panel a bit too well.

Ruth It should have worked. You never know until the tape starts to roll.

Shirley I've been on panels as an expert on many things but never before because my marriage is smashed. Well, that's show-biz. Do let me know if there's anything I can do.

Ruth (*smiling*) I will. Oh, Shirley.

Shirley Yes?

Ruth Supposing it had been Richard?

Shirley (*slightly jokey*) After all he's done to *me*? I'd've said (*slightly mocking the quotation*): "The show must go *on*." (*Seriously*) No. You don't really know. Unless it happens to *you*.

Shirley smiles bitterly and goes

Jean Miss Delahay. I feel I'm—to blame. Really.

Jackie returns to her table and begins writing final comments on her script

Ruth It's a combination of misfortunes. They rarely come in singletons.

Jean Going on about my problems—when her husband was . . .

Ruth Maybe I should have told you. I'd thought it better not to.

Jean If you hadn't stopped because of me, she would have got through, wouldn't she?

Ruth We've had studio crises before. They just don't get on to the screen, so viewers never know.

Caroline returns, putting on a brave face, professionally under control. Wendy comes in behind her

Caroline Oh, have you released everybody? I was going to suggest we have another crack at it.

Ruth You've had enough for today, Caro. We've three in the pipeline, remember.

In the background, Wendy hands Jackie an administrative paper memo in connection with the abandoning of this edition of "Women On View", then exits to the gallery

Jackie puzzles over the paper and decides to refer it to Ruth at a suitable moment

Caroline Mrs Redding, you were very good; wasn't she, Ruth?
Jean Oh, no . . .

Jo comes in R, *takes off Caroline's neck-mike and goes off up to the gallery with it during the following*

Ruth I've been trying to convince her it wasn't her fault.

Caroline One of the best Special Guests we've had, don't you think, Ruth? Apart from that girl, the one who lived with the Hell's Angels. She made marvellous television.

Ruth And the blind girl. She was *very* good. And . . .

Ruth sees Jackie hovering with the administrative note

Yes, Jackie?

Jackie What do we put as reason for abandoning this one?
Ruth Oh, yes. Er—let me see. How to phrase it—so as to, er . . .

Ruth takes Jackie to her table where she sits to write on the note

Caroline Put it all down to me, Ruth. Don't go into details.

Jean wonders if this refers to her part in the proceedings

Jean Miss Power. I'm so sorry. About your husband. If I'd had
the least idea . . .
Caroline Thank you.
Jean I wish there was something I could say. To apologize.
Caroline (*smiling*) Doesn't do any good to talk about it.
Jean No. But I wish I could . . .

*Wendy comes down the gallery steps to Caroline and interrupts
Jean without thought of apology*

Wendy International Press Agency. On the gallery telephone. I
said you might not be able to talk. Should I say you've gone?

*Caroline makes to leave to the gallery. Wendy goes off ahead of
her*

Caroline No, I can talk. Even to the press. (*To Jean*) I wouldn't
compare what's happened today with your situation, Mrs
Redding. It isn't really on, you know, believe me.

Jean looks puzzled, but has no chance to ask for elaboration

Wendy They say, if you could just make a short statement.

*Wendy leads the way up to the gallery. Caroline pauses at the steps
and smiles wryly at Jean*

Caroline See? Not "How is the widow?" Just "make a statement". Like I'd committed a crime. Allowed my husband to
kill himself. When I hadn't seen hide nor hair of him for damn
near six months.

*Caroline exits along the gallery.
Ruth has cleared the administrative problem.
Jackie takes her script and other bits and pieces and goes off* L

Ruth Well, Mrs Redding. It's a pity we won't be seeing you on
transmission next Tuesday.
Jean Oh, it doesn't matter. Better this way, probably. I can see

now. My letter *was* only fit for one of those auntie columns in the paper. And I'd *never* do that, however desperate I got.

Ruth The cruel fact is, no-one can *really* help. It's so personal, we have to work it out for ourselves. Poor Caroline's been using me as a father-confessor since the show started; that's how many weeks? Forty-odd, going on for a year. All I've been able to do is listen; try to sound sympathetic.

Jean (*bemused*) She was just saying—she hadn't seen him . . .

Ruth She and Bob Harvest had gone their separate ways for years. Strong-minded; individualists. Valued their freedom above everything. They fooled themselves they did.

Jean But she was so upset.

Ruth More than she showed. Maybe as much as *you'd* be if it were *your* husband. Or me if it were mine. If you'd seen them together, joking, sparking-off each other, talking incessantly about show-biz in the sort of shorthand two people get into when they know each other right into their hearts. But just because they didn't hit it off, spot on, all the time . . . Instead of agreeing to *dis*agree, they quarrelled, threw things; lived separate lives. Then every now and then there was a great big "all-is-forgiven" lovey-dovey and they were head over heels again. Almost to the point of nausea. That used to last about ten days, and then . . . Oh. Your letter. (*She picks Jean's letter up from the low table and offers it to her*) A memento of "Women On View". Or would you prefer not to be reminded?

Jean I would like to keep it. Thank you. (*She takes the letter*)

Ruth Did you show it to your husband? When you wrote it?

Jean No. No, he was away, on business. Back next week. Oh, I'm going to tell him about being here, but—only that.

Ruth You've not considered discussing the marriage contract with him? Your own contract.

Jean No. I'm scared to. You see—I think it *is* his secretary; corny though it sounds. She . . . travels with him.

Ruth But if he's kept it from you, doesn't that mean *he's* scared, too?

Jean Yes, he probably is; knowing George. But he's getting the best of both worlds, isn't he?

Ruth *If* there is another woman, yes. Men usually do. Why don't you show him that? Tell him what happened today. About Caroline and Bob. It might shake him. Look at Shirley's life, Susanna's—well, in Edna Morton-Smith's word—it's shallow. What Caroline is going to regret, if she isn't already, is what she and Bob threw away. Precious times together. I think you should try answering your own question about the marriage contract. Both of you. Sit down with your husband and read him the small print as you see it. And ask him how he sees it. Then at least you'll know where you stand.

Jean puts the letter in her handbag

Jean Yes, it can't make it any worse. Yes, I must try. I'm not sure George will see *any* small print but you make me want to try. Thank you, Miss Delahay. You've been very . . . (*She can't find the right word*)

Wendy comes down from the gallery

Ruth How is she?

Wendy It's hit her really hard now. She's let the tears come.

Ruth I'll whistle up a car to take her home. Good-bye, Mrs Redding, and thank you. Wendy will take you back to Reception.

Wendy And your husband's on the gallery phone.

Ruth Calling me *here*? What on earth can he want? Today's had its quota of trouble surely.

Ruth sees Jean react to her reaction, and is moved to try and soften it

He makes a point of *never* calling me on studio day. Never.

Ruth goes to the Floor Manager's telephone

Wendy He said it's important. Oh, I told him we've had a write-off.

Ruth (*to Jean*) He knows what that means; he's an accountant. Good-bye, Mrs Redding, and good luck.

Jean Thank you. Good-bye.

Wendy takes Jean off L to the studio door

Ruth (*on the phone*) Ruth Delahay. Give me the call on Gallery

Three B, please . . . Howard? . . . Yes, it's very sad. She wanted to go on but I couldn't let her, then that's Caroline . . . I was just saying to someone here, how happy they could be when they tried . . . What d'you mean, "Do something to-night?" . . . Howard, are you all right? . . . I can't remember when you last offered to take me somewhere as smoochy as that. What about all that backlog of work you're always complaining about . . . I'm not being facetious, of course I'd love to . . . Yes, it has been a hellava day . . . Well, exactly; what *are* we slogging our guts out for, *you* tell me . . . Heavens I've just had a horrible thought; have I forgotten it's our anniversary? No, that's not till . . . I'll go along with that. Yes, why *not* pretend it is? . . . Yes . . .

Wendy enters

(*Seeing Wendy*) I do you, too. When did we last say that to each other! . . . Till then. (*She hangs up, her last words said guardedly and self-consciously now that Wendy has returned*) I'm not hanging about, Wendy. My husband wants to eat at *my* favourite restaurant, how *about* that?

Wendy Fine. I've typed the memo to Programme Controller. Would you sign it before you . . . ?

Ruth Even that can wait until tomorrow. You pack it in for the day, too.

Wendy Thank you.

Ruth makes to go up to the gallery, stops

Ruth You still swanning around with your rugby fanatic?

Wendy He's given up playing. Getting past it, he says.

Ruth More to the point, is he getting tired of asking you to marry him?

Wendy I *still* don't know what to answer. All this today makes me even more confused.

Ruth We can't have everything in life. Cherish the good bits; and try to get through the bad patches.

Wendy (*doubting*) Sounds very difficult.

Ruth Life's more complex and difficult than making television programmes. The trouble is, you only realize it when you look back. By then it's usually too late.

LIGHTS   GO DOWN

They exchange an understanding smile as Wendy goes off to the double doors and Ruth with a last look at the empty chairs, goes on up the gallery steps. The studio is empty

FURNITURE AND PROPERTY LIST

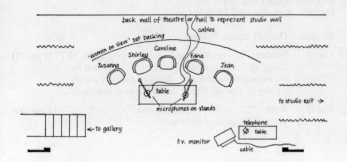

On stage: 5 studio chairs (1 slightly superior)
Low table (below chairs) *On it:* 2 microphones on bases,
letter in envelope, new copy of novel
Small table (off studio "set") *On it:* scripts, telephone
marked with red tape, ball-point pen
TV monitor
Across floor: covered cables and "bridge"

Off stage: Script on clip-board (**Jo**)
Neck-mike connected to portable transmitter and earpiece
(**Jackie**)
Script (**Ruth**)
Tab-marked script on clip-board (**Wendy**)
Neck-mike (**Jo**)
Cue-board (**Jo**)
Paper memo (**Wendy**)

Personal: **Jackie:** watch
Wendy: stop-watch on black tape
Ruth: watch
Jean: handbag

LIGHTING PLOT

Property fittings required: nil
Interior. A studio and TV set

To open: Overall studio lighting

Cue 1   **Shirley:** "... or she never works for you again, eh?" (Page 4)
           *Bring up "set" lighting. This can be suggested by
           removing masking borders and possibly lower-
           ing a row of lights into view over the "set"*

Cue 2   **Ruth:** "... not to worry. Damn!"   (Page 20)
           Return to opening lighting